Pebble® Plus

Royalty

# Castles and Palaces

by Sally Lee

Consulting Editor: Gail Saunders-Smith, PhD

Consultant: Glenn A. Steinberg, PhD
Associate Professor of English
The College of New Jersey
Ewing, New Jersey

CAPSTONE PRESS
a capstone imprint

Pebble Plus is published by Capstone Press,
1710 Roe Crest Drive, North Mankato, Minnesota 56003
www.capstonepub.com

**Library of Congress Cataloging-in-Publication Data**
Lee, Sally.
  Castles and palaces / by Sally Lee.
    pages cm—(Pebble plus. Royalty)
  Includes bibliographical references and index.
  ISBN 978-1-62065-121-6 (library binding)
  ISBN 978-1-4765-1084-2 (eBook PDF)
  1. Castles—Juvenile literature. 2. Palaces—Juvenile literature. I. Title.
  NA7710.L44 2013
  728.8—dc23
                                                    2012030331

**Editorial Credits**
Erika L. Shores, editor; Juliette Peters, designer; Wanda Winch, media researcher; Jennifer Walker, production specialist

**Photo Credits**
Alamy Images: David Parker, 13, Presselect, 15; Corbis: Hemis/Christophe Boisvieux, 11; Getty Images, Inc: WPA Wire/Kieran Doherty, 17; James P. Rowan, 7; Newscom: Zuma Press/Junko Kimura, 19; Shutterstock: Anna Subbotina, red satin design, Dainis Derics, cover, Ecelop, gold swoosh design, hardtmuth, gold frame, Isantilli, 9, Jason Saunders, 21, Markus Gann, 5, St. Nick, 3

## Note to Parents and Teachers

The Royalty set supports national social studies standards related to people, places, and culture. This book describes and illustrates castles and palaces. The images support early readers in understanding the text. The repetition of words and phrases helps early readers learn new words. This book also introduces early readers to subject-specific vocabulary words, which are defined in the Glossary section. Early readers may need assistance to read some words and to use the Table of Contents, Glossary, Read More, Internet Sites, and Index sections of the book.

Printed in China.
092012        006934LEOS13

# Table of Contents

# What Are Castles and Palaces?

How would you like living in

a castle or palace?

Both are grand homes

for royal families

and important leaders.

Hohenzollern Castle,
Hechingen, Germany

Long ago, castles were built

for protection, not comfort.

They were hard to heat

and had few windows

for fresh air and sunlight.

Bodiam Castle,
East Sussex, England

7

Unlike castles, palaces were built for comfort. Today castle homes are as grand as palaces. Some castles and palaces have become museums or hotels.

Louvre Museum,
Paris, France

9

# A Look Inside

Palaces and castles can have hundreds of rooms. Some are for the family's living quarters.

Glamis Castle,
Angus, Scotland

11

Fancy palace rooms have different uses. Ballrooms are perfect for large parties. Smaller groups meet in drawing rooms.

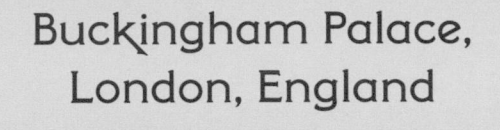

Buckingham Palace,
London, England

Huge palaces are still being built.

The world's largest palace is

in Brunei. It has 1,788 rooms,

257 bathrooms, and

a 110-car garage.

Istana Nurul Iman Palace,
Bandar Seri Begawan, Brunei

# Famous Castles and Palaces

England's Queen Elizabeth II has several homes. One is Windsor Castle near London. It has a room with a table and chairs for 160 dinner guests.

The Emperor of Japan lives
in the Imperial Palace in Tokyo.
People gather outside to see
the royal family.

Neuschwanstein Castle is

in the mountains of Germany.

Fairy-tale castles have been

made to look like Neuschwanstein.

Say it like this:
Neuschwanstein
(noy-SHVAN-shtine)

# Glossary

**Brunei** (broon-EYE)—a small, oil-rich country on the South China Sea

**drawing room**—a room in a house used for visiting with guests

**emperor**—the male ruler of an empire or group of nations; an empire is a large area of land ruled by a powerful leader

**imperial**—having to do with an empire or an emperor

**museum**—a building where people can see objects important to history, art, or science

**protection**—the act of keeping something safe from harm

# Read More

**Lee, Sally.** *Kings and Queens.* Royalty. North Mankato, Minn.: Capstone Press, 2013.

**Stiefel, Chana.** *Ye Castle Stinketh: Could You Survive Living in a Castle?* Ye Yucky Middle Ages. Berkeley Heights, N.J.: Enslow, 2012.

**Weil, Ann.** *The World's Most Amazing Castles.* Landmark Top Tens. Chicago: Raintree, 2012.

# Internet Sites

FactHound offers a safe, fun way to find Internet sites related to this book. All of the sites on FactHound have been researched by our staff.

Here's all you do:

Visit *www.facthound.com*

Type in this code: 9781620651216

# Index

Word Count: 185
Grade: 1
Early-Intervention Level: 20